MW01264461

I can help Others

Written by
**Rhonda Reeves and
Jennifer Law**

Illustrated by
Timothy Robinson

**Woman's Missionary Union
Birmingham, AL 35283-0010**

Published by Woman's Missionary Union, SBC
P.O. Box 830010
Birmingham, AL 35283-0010

©1998 by Woman's Missionary Union, SBC
All rights reserved. First printing 1998
Printed in China
Woman's Missionary Union® and WMU® are registered trademarks

Dewey Decimal Classification: CE
Subject Headings: CHRISTIAN LIFE–CHILDREN
                  HELPING BEHAVIOR
                  CHILDREN'S LITERATURE

Series: Missions and Me

ISBN: 1-56309-255-7
W988105•088•05M1

God made different kinds of people.

People can help each other.

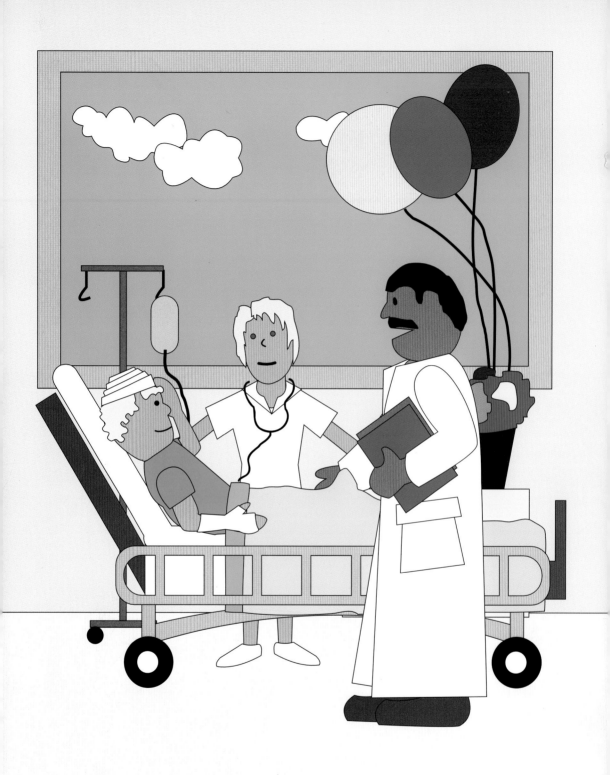

Some people help the sick.

I can help the sick, too.

3rd Avenue Shelter

Some give food to people who are hungry.

I can help hungry people, too.

Some people teach others about God.

I can tell others about God, too.

Some people pray for others.

I can pray for others, too.

God wants us to help others.